**Dear Parents and Teachers,**

In an easy-reader format, **My Readers** introduce classic stories to children who are learning to read. Nonfiction **My Readers** tell true stories and convey fascinating facts to children who are ready to read on their own.

My Readers are available in three levels:

1 **Level One** is for the emergent reader and features repetitive language and word clues in the illustrations.

2 **Level Two** is for more advanced readers who still need support saying and understanding some words. Stories are longer with word clues in the illustrations.

3 **Level Three** is for independent, fluent readers who enjoy working out occasional unfamiliar words. The stories are longer and divided into chapters.

Encourage children to select books based on interests, not reading levels. Read aloud with children, showing them how to use the illustrations for clues. With adult guidance and rereading, children will eventually read the desired book on their own.

Here are some ways you might want to use this book with children:

- Talk about the title and the cover illustrations. Encourage the child to use these to predict what the story is about.
- Discuss the interior illustrations and try to piece together a story based on the pictures. Does the child want to change or adjust his first prediction?
- After children reread a story, suggest they retell or act out a favorite part.

My Readers will not only help children become readers, they will serve as an introduction to some of the finest classic children's books available today.

—LAURA ROBB
Educator and Reading Consultant

For activities and reading tips, visit myreadersonline.com.

To all my writer and illustrator friends
who continually fill me with creative ideas and wisdom.

With thanks to Sally Doherty, Amy Allen, and Véronique Sweet for their inspired and creative work on this book.

PHOTO CREDITS: cover, page 6, 7: Brenda Z. Guiberson; page 8: R. Dale Guthrie; page 3, 20-21: University of Alaska Museum; page 22: Neg. no. 411970, courtesy of the Department of Library Services, American Museum of Natural History; page 24: Neg. no. 310539, courtesy of the Department of Library Services, American Museum of Natural History; page 34-35: Courtesy of National Park Service, Chaco Culture National Historical Park; page 44: Western History Collections, University of Oklahoma Libraries, Rose 2065

SQUARE
FISH

An Imprint of Macmillan Children's Publishing Group

Library of Congress Cataloging-in-Publication Data Available

ISBN 978-0-8050-8976-9 (hardcover)
1 3 5 7 9 10 8 6 4 2

ISBN 978-1-250-01047-6 (paperback)
1 3 5 7 9 10 8 6 4 2

Book design by Patrick Collins/Véronique Lefèvre Sweet

Square Fish logo designed by Filomena Tuosto
Originally published by Henry Holt and Company, 1998
First MY READERS Edition: 2013

myreadersonline.com
mackids.com

This is a Level 3 book

Lexile 580L

Mummy
Mysteries

TALES FROM NORTH AMERICA

BRENDA Z. GUIBERSON

SQUARE
FISH

Macmillan Children's Publishing Group
New York

GLOSSARY

ARSENIC: A chemical that can be used to stop a dead animal or plant from rotting away.

BISON: This largest land mammal in North America is often called a buffalo. Blue Babe was a steppe bison, an ancestor of the modern plains and wood bison of today.

DECAY: The action of a dead animal or plant as it breaks down and rots away.

HISTORIAN: Someone who studies or writes about events from the past.

INVESTIGATE: To make a careful study of details and clues.

MIDDEN: A pile of seeds, leaves, bones, or other remains gathered by a pack rat. It can also be an old trash heap left behind by ancient people.

MINERAL: A non-living material found in the earth that is the same all the way through. Two or more minerals together make a rock.

MUMMY: A dead body with its organs and tissues preserved.

ORGANS: Many tissues working together to do the same job become an organ. The heart, lungs, skin, kidneys, and brain are some of the organs of a body.

PRESERVE: To protect from decay and rot.

PREY: Animals that are hunted and eaten by other animals.

PUEBLO: A Spanish word that means "town" or "village" and is used to describe communities of Native Americans in the Southwest United States.

PUNCTURE: To make a small hole by poking with a sharp or pointed object.

SIDESHOW: A small show at a circus or carnival that is offered in addition to the main event.

TIME CAPSULE: A collection of items or information preserved with the hope that others will learn from them in the future.

TISSUES: A group of cells, like muscle cells, that work together, such as muscle tissue.

WATER JET: A high-powered blast of water that can cut or carve into metal, rock, or permafrost.

WEAVERS: People who bend, shape, and twist plant fibers into items such as baskets, sandals, and fabrics.

WILLOW: A low-growing plant eaten by bison. This plant can be used by weavers to make baskets and fish traps.

CONTENTS

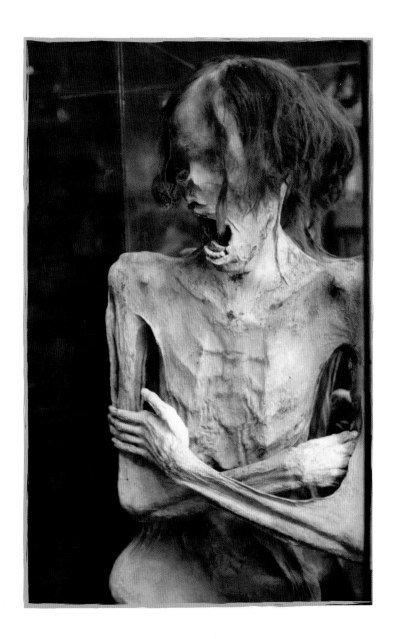

IS THAT A MUMMY?

Mummies are real.

They are dead people or animals

protected from decay.

Skeletons are only bones.

Mummies have preserved

hair, skin, muscle, and organs.

If we look carefully at them,

mummies can solve

mysteries from the past.

CHAPTER TWO

THE MYSTERY OF BLUE BABE

Pearl Creek, Alaska, 1979

Walter Roman is looking for gold.

He uses a powerful water jet

to wash away dirt

frozen for thousands of years.

Then he finds something unusual.

He sees a hoof and hairy legs.

He sees horns.

He has discovered a mummy!

He calls scientists to investigate.

Scientists study the layers of dirt
above the mummy.
They discover that it is a male bison
who died about 36,000 years ago.

10

He is covered with a mineral
that looks blue.
They call him Blue Babe.
Because bison no longer live in Alaska,
everyone is excited to learn more.

The scientists count the rings
on his horns.
They study the food stuck
between his teeth.

These clues reveal that Blue Babe
was about 8 years old
and ate grass and willow.

They note his heavy fur
and thick layer of fat.
These clues mean that Blue Babe died
in fall or early winter.
This is the time when bison
grow more fur and eat extra food
to prepare for cold winters.

Blue Babe's hide has scratch marks
made by very sharp claws.
His head has puncture marks
made by long teeth.
A large animal, perhaps two,
attacked Blue Babe.
But which animal?

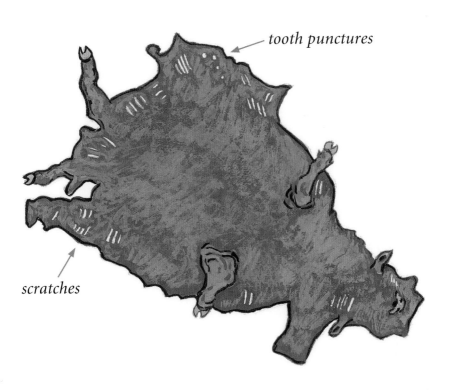

tooth punctures

scratches

The scratch marks couldn't come
from a bear.

Bear claws are used for digging.
They are not sharp enough.

Could it be wolves?

No, they do not use claws
to catch prey.
Their teeth are too narrow
to make these puncture marks.

What about the saber-toothed tiger?

No, it had teeth
that sliced like a knife.
None of these animals
killed Blue Babe.

The clues show that one large animal
pulled Blue Babe down from behind.
Another large animal attacked
Blue Babe's head.
This is the way lions hunt.
Lions do not live in Alaska today.
But did they live with Blue Babe
36,000 years ago?

Then scientists find a chipped tooth

stuck in his neck.

It is a lion's tooth.

The mystery of Blue Babe's death
is solved.

CHAPTER THREE
MYSTERY OF THE ANASAZI

Ancient Deserted Cities,
Southwest United States, 1890s

Old ruins of great abandoned cities

are discovered in a desert.

These ruins are from the Anasazi.

The Anasazi people came

to the Southwest

over two thousand years ago.

Who were the Anasazi?

What happened to them?

It is a mystery.

Scientists dig and sift for clues.

They find mummies

with woven sandals and baskets.

The Anasazi were clever weavers.

Scientists find dried squash seeds,

beans, and corncobs, too.

The Anasazi were good farmers.

They did not have to wander

in search of food.

They stayed in one area and

built amazing places to live.

Without wheels, metal tools,
or large animals to help,
they hauled in 200,000 mountain trees
to build their cities, called pueblos.
The largest, Pueblo Bonito,
grew to include hundreds of rooms.

It was the largest apartment house

in the world until 1882.

Mummies can tell us

who the Anasazi were,

but what happened to them?

It's a mystery.

In the 1200s, the Anasazi left.
Why would hardworking people build
great cities and then abandon them?

The mummies can't tell us,
but there are other clues.
Pack rats lived in the dry caves
before the Anasazi came.
They stayed after the Anasazi left.

Pack rats like to collect things

for their nests.

For thousands of years,

pack rats collected feathers and seeds,

juniper cones and pinecones,

and nearby insects, too.

The dry air of the desert

preserved the nests.

Some are thousands of years old.

When scientists pull apart old nests,

called pack-rat middens,

they find new Anasazi clues.

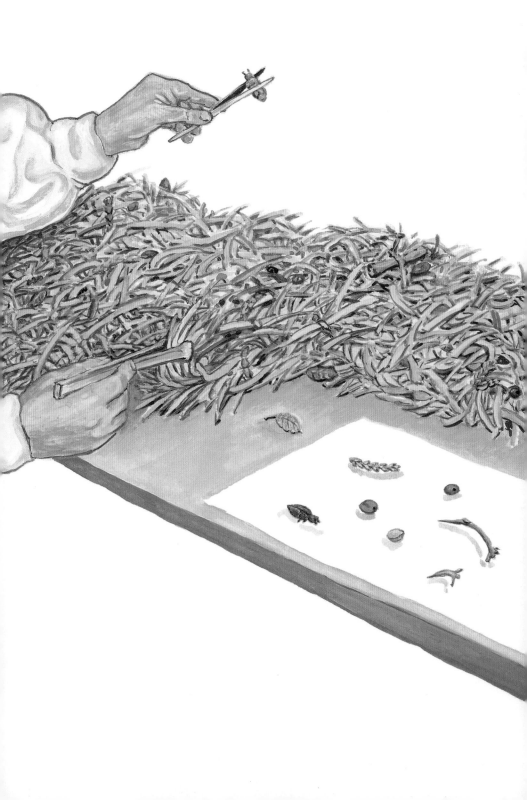

A thousand years ago,

juniper and pine trees

grew around Pueblo Bonito.

Pack rats collected the cones.

But over the next 200 years,

the Anasazi expanded

and cut down more trees.

The pack rats collected

fewer cones.

Then there were no cones at all.

What happened?

It was a time of little rain.

The Anasazi needed trees

for building and for fuel.

More and more trees disappeared.

The plants and animals that depended on trees disappeared, too.

Did the Anasazi leave Pueblo Bonito because the trees were gone?

It's still a mystery today.

CHAPTER FOUR

THE OUTLAW WHO WOULDN'T GIVE UP

Long Beach, California, 1976

A dummy is hanging in a fun house.

Somebody decides to move it.

They reach for the dummy.

Plunk! The arm falls off.

It has a real bone.

This dummy is a mummy.

But who is it?

And how did it get there?

Another mummy mystery begins.

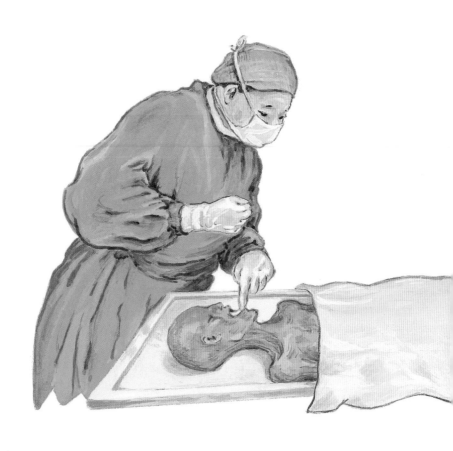

A doctor studies the bones and tissues.

This mummy was a man

about 30 years old.

A copper bullet is in his chest.

It was made between 1830

and World War 1.

The doctor looks in the mummy's mouth.
He finds a 1924 copper penny.
He also finds a ticket stub
from a "Museum of Crime."

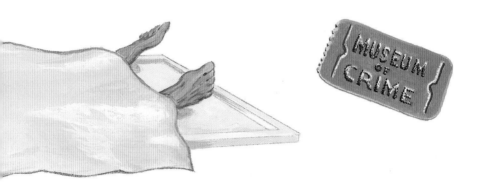

The museum owner's son says his father
bought the mummy in the 1920s.
He thought it was a dummy.
People paid twenty-five cents to see
"the outlaw who wouldn't give up."
Later the mummy was bought
and sold many times.

Now the mummy needs a name.

A police investigation reveals

that the mummy was from Oklahoma.

Historians in that state

find a likely suspect.

The mummy might be Elmer McCurdy.

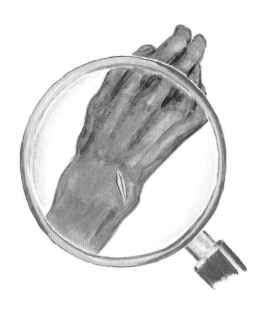

Elmer McCurdy was about the same age

and height as the mummy.

He was a robber.

Prison records describe

a two-inch scar on his right wrist.

The California mummy has the same

two-inch scar on the right wrist.

Now the mummy has a name

and a story.

Elmer was part of a gang

that robbed a train.

The robbers picked the wrong train.

They got only $46 and some whiskey.

Elmer drank the whiskey

and fell asleep in a hayloft.

The sheriff found him.

Elmer refused to give up.

He was killed by a copper bullet.

Elmer's body was preserved
with a chemical called arsenic.
Everyone forgot he was Elmer.
He spent 66 years in sideshows,
circuses, and the fun house.
Finally, the mummy was buried
in Oklahoma in 1977.

CHAPTER FIVE
LOOKING
FOR MUMMIES

———•———

There are many mysteries in our world.

Mummies can solve some of them.

Mummies are like time capsules

guarding mysterious information.

Looking for mummies is like

being a good detective.

Find the subject, preserve the scene,

and read the clues.

Mummy mysteries are waiting to be solved.

MORE MUMMIES

This baby mammoth
tells us many things
about an animal
that no longer exists.

This bog mummy is
well-preserved and
still has whiskers.

The Egyptians made
millions of mummies,
including some from cats.
Today scientists can study
these wrapped mummies
with X-rays.

INDEX